Some Assembly Required Workbook

How to Make, Grow, and Keep Your Relationships

www.networkingquotient.com

Copyright © 2010
New Year Publishing, LLC
144 Diablo Ranch Ct.
Danville, CA 94506 USA

orders@newyearpublishing.com
http://www.newyearpublishing.com

All rights reserved.

ISBN 978-09671565-2-1

Networking Myths

1. Networking is only for times when you are not busy. TRUE FALSE

2. Only senior executives need to network. TRUE FALSE

3. The people you meet networking never refer you business. TRUE FALSE

4. Networking is not necessary because if you are really good, the business will find you. TRUE FALSE

5. Decision makers never attend networking events. TRUE FALSE

Four Reasons To Network With Your Competition

1. _____

2. _____

3. _____

4. _____

Anyone Can Refer Business

Make a list of the top 5 people who have referred you business in the last year:

NAME	INDUSTRY
1.	
2.	
3.	
4.	
5.	

Make a list of five other people from the above industries that you might want to get to know better, who could become referral sources.

1. _____

2. _____

3. _____

4. _____

5. _____

List your top ten clients, how you first found them, and what other services you could sell to them.

Company	Business Development Method	Cross-Selling Opportunities
1.		
2.		
3.		
4.		
5.		
6.		
7.		
8.		
9.		
10.		

Wish List

Quickly list 50 companies you would like as clients.

Company	Company
1.	13.
2.	14.
3.	15.
4.	16.
5.	17.
6.	18.
7.	19.
8.	20.
9.	21.
10.	22.
11.	23.
12.	24.

Company	Company
25.	38.
26.	39.
27.	40.
28.	41.
29.	42.
30.	43.
31.	44.
32.	45.
33.	46.
34.	47.
35.	48.
36.	49.
37.	50.

Target List

Prioritize your top 20 targets.

Company	Existing Contact?	Priority (A / B / C)
1.		
2.		
3.		
4.		
5.		
6.		
7.		
8.		
9.		
10.		
11.		
12.		
13		
14.		
15.		
16.		
17.		
18.		
19.		
20.		

Personal Career Goals

List 5 career goals you would like to accomplish

1. _____

2. _____

3. _____

4. _____

5. _____

Regularly review the goals you listed. Without knowing where you want to go, it is hard to be motivated to network with the people who can help you achieve. If you are focused on what you want, then it is easier to network.

Helping Others

Make a list of five people who you have helped in their career in the past month.

1. _____

2. _____

3. _____

4. _____

5. _____

If you want those in your network to help you reach your goals, you must regularly discover ways to assist other people. To establish long lasting, mutually beneficial relationships you must lead by example

First Impressions

List reasons why each of the below matter to the people you meet:

1. Appearance: _____

2. Firm Handshake _____

3. Eye Contact _____

4. Not trying to sell immediately _____

_____

Online Social Networking

Important things to remember about your online activities:

1. _____

2. _____

3. _____

4. _____

5. _____

6. _____

7. _____

8. _____

Online networking does not replace face-to-face networking. They are all connected and part of establishing your brand. A powerful network takes time and effort to establish.

Tools of the trade

The little things make the difference. Make notes as to why each of the following are important:

Asking Questions _____

_____

Business cards _____

_____

Nametags _____

_____

Stationary _____

_____

LinkedIn Profile_____

_____

Database/CRM _____

_____

Unique events _____

_____

Public Speaking Skills _____

_____

Writing Articles _____

_____

Client Surveys _____

_____

Having a Mentor_____

_____

Being a Mentor _____

_____

Knowing Current Events _____

_____

Volunteering _____

_____

Educating Others About Your Ideal Client _____

_____

 www.networkingquotient.com

1. How do you view the importance of networking in your business life?

    a. a waste of time

    b. important, but rarely a priority

    c. very important

2. Do you have an elevator statement / signature story?

    a. what?

    b. I have an understanding of what these are.

    c. I have an elevator statement and signature stories, and can clearly articulate it to anyone.

3. In the past 12 months I have attended industry conferences, local networking events and seminars.

    a. None; I don't have time and money.

    b. 1 to 5

    c. 6 to eleven or more

    d. More than once a month I attend networking events.

4. When I meet someone who could be a client or important business contact

    a. I always follow up within a few days with an email or handwritten note.

    b. I sometimes follow up if we discussed something important.

    c. I mean to follow up, but rarely do a good job of it.

5. When I meet someone new I ask for a business card.

    a. always

    b. sometimes, if it seems appropriate

    c. rarely

6. When I make a connection with someone new, I schedule a follow up visit within two weeks.

    a. always

    b. sometimes

    c. never

    d. I wait for them to call me.

7. The word "networking"

    a. makes me cringe.

    b. is just a word.

    c. is an important part of my business life.

8. How many business books do you read in a year?

    a. 0-1

    b. 2-5

    c. 5-10

    d. 10+

9. I share my business goals with members of my network.

    Yes / No

10. When I meet someone new, I am conscious of the importance of a first impression.

    Yes / No

11. I look for unique opportunities to interact with clients and prospects.

    Yes / No

12. I regularly set business goals that include developing new business relationships.

    Yes / No

13. I view my competitors as

    a. evil.

    b. annoying.

    c. just there.

    d. more people who could be part of my network.

14. I put information of everyone I meet into my contact database.

    Yes / No

15. I work hard to build strong networking relationships internally in my organiza-tion, not just with those outside my company.

    Yes / No

16. When I meet someone new in the business community I

    a. look for ways they can help my business.

    b. look for ways I can help their business without concern for what they do for me.

    c. think that networking is a 50/50 give and tak.e

17. The way I feel about speaking and making business presentations can be categorized as:

    a. I look for opportunities and feel comfortable speaking in public.

    b. I do not look forward to it, but can manage when I have to.

    c. I do not speak in public, as it does not effect my career.

18. I subscribe to at least one of the Online Social Networking sites(example: LinkedIn, Facebook, Twitter, Plaxo, ecademy, MySpace, Orkut, etc...)

    a. I don't.

    b. One of them

    c. More than one

    d. Yes, and I utilize them several times a week.

19. I am seen as a resource that is willing to help others by everyone in my network?

    a. "Everyone" is such a big term.

    b. Most people would agree with that statement.

    c. I don't have time to help others.

20. I enjoy helping people achieve their goals even if I get nothing from the gesture.

    Yes / No

21. If I was laid off from my current job, I feel confident I could find employment opportunities

    a. within a month.

    b. in 2-5 months.

    c. within a year.

    d. I have no idea, thinking about this scares me to death.

22. Making time for networking is for when you are not busy with other projects.

    True False

23. Networking is not important if you are the best in your field.

    True /False

24. I have a written target list of the top ten prospects I want as clients.

    Yes / No

25. When I meet a potential client for the first time I:

    a. Immediately tell them about my product/service.

    b. Try to set an appointment to sell them.

    c. Realize that a first meeting is just that, and try to engage them in conversation to identify areas of common interest.

26. When I do a favor for someone else I expect them to do the same for me

    Yes / No

27. At least once a month I look at my contact database and find ways to assist others.

    Yes / No

28. I believe the following makes a difference in how people view me.

    a. a firm handshake and eye contact

    b. my appearance (clothes and grooming)

    c. Being well informed about current events (both in business and pop culture)

    d. all of the above

    e. None of that matters.

29. I routinely follow up with new people I meet.

    Yes / No

30. When someone does me a favor I always send a thank you note or other token of appreciation.

    Yes / No

31. I view online social networking sites like MySpace, Facebook and LinkedIn as:

    a. A fad.

    b. Complicated.

    c. A useful tool that can help me maintain and create new relationships.

    d. A fast way to make real connections for business.

32. Have you ever read any of the books in The Some Assembly Required series or seen the live seminar presentation?

    Yes / No

33. When I read a magazine article or blog post that I know would interest other people I

    a. Cut it out and mail it to them or forward the digital link.

    b. Tell them about the article.

    c. I do nothing.

34. When someone sends me a magazine article or blog post that they thought would interest me I think:

    a. Wow, that was very thoughtful and an above average gesture.

    b. I am indifferent.

    c. I wonder why they don't have something better to do with their time than forwarding me articles.

Scoring key

Question	Answer / Choice	Points	Your Score
1	a	-1	
	b	-1	
	c	2	
2	a	-1	
	b	0	
	c	2	
3	a	-1	
	b	0	
	c	1	
	d	2	
4	a	2	
	b	1	
	c	-1	
5	a	2	
	b	1	
	c	-1	
6	a	2	
	b	1	
	c	-1	
	d	-2	
7	a	-2	
	b	0	
	c	2	
Column 1 total:			

Question	Answer / Choice	Points	Your Score
8	a	-1	
	b	0	
	c	1	
	d	2	
9	Yes	2	
	No	-1	
10	Yes	2	
	No	-1	
11	Yes	2	
	No	-1	
12	Yes	2	
	No	-1	
13	a	-1	
	b	-1	
	c	0	
	d	2	
14	Yes	2	
	No	-1	
15	Yes	1	
	No	-1	
16	a	-2	
	b	2	
	c	1	
Column 2 total:			

Scoring key

Question	Answer / Choice	Points	Your Score
17	a	2	
	b	1	
	c	-1	
18	a	-1	
	b	1	
	c	2	
	d	3	
19	a	0	
	b	1	
	c	-1	
20	Yes	1	
	No	-1	
21	a	2	
	b	1	
	c	0	
	d	-2	
22	True	-1	
	False	2	
23	True	-1	
	False	2	
24	Yes	2	
	No	-1	
	Column 3 total:		

Question	Answer / Choice	Points	Your Score
25	a	-1	
	b	0	
	c	2	
26	Yes	-1	
	No	2	
27	Yes	2	
	No	-1	
28	a	1	
	b	1	
	c	1	
	d	2	
	e	-2	
29	Yes	2	
	No	-1	
30	Yes	2	
	No	-1	
31	a	-1	
	b	-1	
	c	2	
	d	-1	
	Column 4 total:		

Scoring key

Question	Answer / Choice	Points	Your Score
32	Yes	2	
	No	0	
33	a	2	
	b	0	
	c	-1	
34	a	1	
	b	0	
	c	-1	
	Column 5 total:		
	Column 4 total:		
	Column 3 total:		
	Column 2 total:		
	Column 1 total:		
	TOTAL:		

Scoring key

The current highest possible total is 66 points. The following ranges will let you know how your networking skills are categorized by all the surveys in our database.

55-66 POINTS: Expert Networker. You are obviously doing the things right to make, grow and keep your business relationships. You have embraced networking as a lifestyle, and clearly understand the benefits to cultivating your social networking connections. You make the other people in your business and personal life a priority and look for ways to be a resource to those around you. Your rewards will be many. Keep up the good work and Never Stop Networking!

44-54 POINTS: Good Networking Skills. You are on the right track with your networking, but it would be beneficial to your career if you made your professional network more of a priority. Your score proves that you realize the people who make up your social and professional network are not just supporting players, but have lead roles in your current and future success. You only need to make some minor adjustments to take your business relationships to the next level.

33-43 POINTS: Needs Some Improvement. Your score shows that you have not fully embraced the importance of social networking in your career. People do business with people they know and like, and your increased attention to building relationships will benefit you in many ways. Look for ways to be a resource for others and to let them know that you care as much about them and their success as you do about your own. The effort that you put into building your network will come back to you in ways you have not imagined.

BELOW 32 POINTS: Networking Not A Priority. Your score shows that you do not view building and maintaining professional relationships as important to your current or future business success. Since people tend to to business with people they know and like, you could benefit from spending more time thinking about your clients, coworkers and prospects and look for ways to become a beneficial resource for them, so that they can respond with more business and referrals.

www.ingramcontent.com/pod-product-compliance
Lightning Source LLC
Chambersburg PA
CBHW081300170426
43198CB00017B/2864